PROXIMITY

How Where You Are Determines Who You Become

The Hidden Force Behind Your Relationships, Career, Health, Wealth, Beliefs, and Everything In Between

Rob Gallant & Bert Medlock
Co-Authors

First Edition, 2025

ISBN: 979-8-9963374-1-5

Printed in the United States of America

Contents

Foreword

This book has been a long time coming. Longer than either of us would care to admit.

The idea belongs to Bert. It had been living inside him for years, turning over quietly in the background of his thinking the way a genuinely good idea does when it has not yet found its moment. The concept was deceptively simple: that proximity, the physical and social circumstances of where you are, does more to shape a life than talent, character, or individual will. Bert had traced it across relationships, careers, faith, wealth, health. He had seen it everywhere. And he had long harbored the ambition to write it all down.

The concept began surfacing in conversations between Bert and Rob. At first it appeared the way big ideas often do in good conversation: sideways, embedded in some other discussion, recognizable only in retrospect as the thing that was really being talked about. Why do people end up with the partners they end up with? Why does success seem to cluster in certain cities, certain schools, certain rooms? Why do two people of equal ability, born in different places, arrive at such different lives? Bert had answers. He always came back to the same word.

Proximity.

Rob found the framework compelling from the start. And so, as years passed and the book remained unwritten, Rob did what a good friend and collaborator does: he nudged. Gently at first. Then with some regularity. "You should write the book, Bert." A year later: "How about now?" Another year: "Seriously, what are you waiting for?" The nudges became a running thread between them, a minor refrain in an otherwise wide-ranging friendship. Bert always had reasons. The timing was not quite right. The framing needed more thought. There was more to consider.

Eventually, Rob stopped waiting.

He sat down and wrote the book himself, channeling years of conversation, Bert's original framework, and his own conviction that the idea deserved to exist in the world. When the draft landed in Bert's hands, something shifted. The concept he had carried so long was suddenly, undeniably real. Bert dug in, sharpened the arguments, added depth where the thinking needed it, and pushed back where the draft had not yet earned its conclusions. The book you are holding is better for that process than either of them could have produced alone.

There is, of course, a certain irony in all of this. A book about how proximity shapes outcomes was itself shaped by proximity: by the specific friendship of two specific people, by the conversations only that combination could have produced, and by the particular kind of creative pressure that only comes from being known well enough that someone refuses to let your best idea quietly expire.

We hope it was worth the wait. We rather think it was.

Rob Gallant
Bert Medlock
Co-Authors

Preface: The Force You Never Noticed

"Proximity has as much influence as God."
Anonymous

There is a force shaping your life so pervasive, so omnipresent, that it has become invisible to you. It guided you to your partner, directed you to your career, sculpted your beliefs, determined your health outcomes, and set the ceiling on your wealth. It is not fate. It is not God. It is not talent alone. It is proximity.

Most of us walk through life believing in the mythology of the self-made individual; the idea is our choices, our character, and our unique destiny are the primary architects of our lives. We tell ourselves that we married our soul mate because the universe conspired to bring two perfect people together. We believe we got our dream job because we were the best candidate. We assume we believe what we believe because we arrived at those conclusions through reason and reflection. We think we are healthy or unhealthy because of the personal decisions we make each day.

This book will systematically dismantle those comfortable fictions. Not to be cruel. Not to rob you of meaning. But to hand you something far more powerful than mythology: clarity. Because when you see the true force driving your outcomes, you can, for the first time, consciously work with it, or deliberately work against it.

The argument of this book is simple, even if its implications are vast: in nearly every domain of human life, your outcomes are determined less by who you are and more by where you are. Proximity (physical, social, intellectual, and digital) is the master variable.

Consider a few opening facts before we begin. Research consistently shows that most married couples live within a few miles of each other before they meet. Studies of elite athletes reveal they predominantly come from specific zip codes. Nobel Prize winners cluster in a handful of universities. Billionaires concentrate in specific cities. The language you speak, the religion you practice, the political party you support, the food you eat, the diseases you are most likely to contract, and the age at which you are likely to die. All of these correlate more strongly with geography than with genetics, character, or divine plan.

"Tell me where you were born, where you went to school, and where you live now. I can tell you more about your life outcomes than you can tell me yourself."

This book is organized around the major domains of human existence. In each chapter, we will examine a different dimension of life and show how proximity has been the silent master of the game. We will look at relationships, education, careers, health, wealth, religion, language, culture, crime, happiness, politics, and opportunity.

By the end, you will have a new lens through which to see your life. You will understand why the most important decision you may ever make is not who to marry, or what career to choose, but rather where to position yourself on this planet. You will see that luck, that most misunderstood of concepts, is largely a function of geography. And you will understand the profound responsibility and opportunity that comes with that knowledge.

Let us begin.

Chapter One: Love Is a Radius

"I fell in love with her the moment I saw her across the room. It was destiny."
Virtually everyone, about a relationship forged by geography

The Myth of the Soul Mate

The concept of the soul mate is among the most persistent and cherished fictions in human culture. It holds that somewhere on this earth, or in the cosmos at large, there exists a single perfect person who was made for you. The universe, in its infinite wisdom, is conspiring to bring you together. Your meeting was inevitable. Your love was written in the stars.

It is a beautiful idea. It is also, mathematically, absurd.

There are approximately 8 billion people alive on Earth today. If we conservatively apply basic compatibility filters (age within a decade, shared language, broad cultural overlap, sexual orientation), we are left with hundreds of millions of potential compatible partners for virtually any individual alive. The notion that the universe has selected one specific person out of those hundreds of millions, and arranged for you to meet them in your city, in your school, in your workplace, or in your neighborhood, strains credulity to the breaking point.

What actually happened is simpler and more honest: you met the people near you, and you married the best of those. Proximity, not providence, wrote your love story.

The Mathematics of Meeting

The statistics on this point are not subtle. A landmark study published in the American Sociological Review found that couples who eventually marry were, on average, living within a few miles of each other when they first met. Researchers studying marriage patterns in Philadelphia in the early twentieth century found that one-third of all couples who married had been living within five city blocks of one another before their first date.

This was not a quirk of an earlier, less mobile era. A 2019 Stanford University study by sociologist Michael Rosenfeld tracked how couples meet in the modern age. It found that the most common way couples meet is still through mutual friends; that is, people within shared social proximity. Online dating, which has dramatically expanded the theoretical pool of potential partners, still tends to match people who live within reasonable driving distance of one another. We may have expanded the radius slightly, but we have not escaped it.

PROXIMITY IN ROMANCE

~50% of married couples

met their spouse within a few miles of their residence, through school, workplace, neighborhood, or mutual local friends. Long-distance cosmic destiny had nothing to do with it.

The workplace and the university are, statistically, the most powerful matchmaking machines ever devised, not because they select for romantic compatibility, but because they concentrate people of similar age, educational background, and ambition in a shared physical space for prolonged periods of time. This creates the conditions for proximity to do its work.

The mere exposure effect, a well-documented psychological phenomenon first described by Robert Zajonc, tells us that repeated exposure to a person increases our liking of them, independent of any meaningful interaction. We are literally wired to develop affection for those we encounter repeatedly. Your coworker becomes attractive to you in part because you see them every day. Your neighbor becomes interesting because your paths cross regularly. The person you keep running into at the coffee shop becomes, over time, someone you want to know better.

"We don't fall in love with the best person on Earth. We fall in love with the best person in our radius."

The Population Argument

Let us be blunt about what the soul mate myth ignores: the sheer scale of human population. China has over 1.4 billion people. India has over 1.4 billion. Together, those two nations account for more than 35 percent of all human beings alive on this planet. If the universe were truly sending you a predetermined partner, the statistical probability is that your soul mate is farming rice in Jiangxi Province or running a textile business in Tamil Nadu.

You did not meet them. You will never meet them. Not because the universe failed you, but because you live in Cincinnati or Manchester or Nairobi, and you met the people who also live in Cincinnati or Manchester or Nairobi.

This is not a tragedy. The person you married or partnered with is real, is valuable, and loves you genuinely. The relationship is no less meaningful for being proximity-forged. But the honesty matters, because it changes how we understand luck, access, and the quality of our options. Someone who grew up in a small rural town of 2,000 people had fundamentally fewer romantic options than someone who grew up in a city of 2 million. This is not a reflection on either person's worth. It is an arithmetic fact with real consequences.

Social Proximity and Class Endogamy

The proximity effect in relationships extends beyond geography into social strata. A consistent finding in sociology is that people marry within their own social class, educational level, and income bracket at remarkably high rates. Ivy League graduates marry other Ivy League graduates. Children of professionals marry other professionals' children. Working-class communities largely reproduce within their social tier.

This is not primarily because people consciously discriminate against those of different backgrounds. It is because they rarely encounter them. Universities sort by academic achievement, which correlates with family income. Neighborhoods sort by housing cost. Workplaces sort by credential and industry. The result is that social proximity creates a self-reinforcing loop: you are most likely to partner with someone whose background resembles yours, not because similarity was your romantic criterion, but because it was the demographic reality of your immediate world.

The implications for social mobility are significant. If your parents were poor, you are likely to grow up in a poor neighborhood, attend under-resourced schools, and socialize primarily with other people in similar circumstances. Your romantic options, your proximity pool, will largely consist of people facing the same structural barriers. The brilliant, ambitious person a few zip codes away, in a different social world, might be a transformative partner who accelerates your trajectory. But proximity says: you will not meet them.

Digital Proximity: The New Radius

The rise of online dating has done something fascinating: it has made digital proximity the new geographical proximity. Dating apps present profiles algorithmically: they show you people who are nearby, who share demographic characteristics, who have similar interests. In effect, they replicate the sorting mechanisms of physical proximity in digital space.

Moreover, even when apps technically allow global matching, people consistently choose partners they can physically reach. Commuting radius, cultural familiarity, and shared time zones still dominate romantic choice even when the theoretical options are global. We have not escaped proximity. We have digitized it.

The lesson is this: if you want to change your romantic outcomes, the most powerful thing you can do is not work on yourself, though that certainly helps. It is to change your physical and social proximity; move to a city with a larger, more compatible population, to join communities, organizations, and environments that concentrate people with aligned values and interests. You are not searching the universe for your perfect match. You are drawing from the pool in front of you. Make the pool larger.

Chapter Two: The School at the End of Your Street

"Education is the great equalizer."
Horace Mann, 1848, who could not have anticipated zip codes

The Promise and the Reality

Every society tells its children a foundational story about education: that it is the great equalizer, the meritocratic ladder by which anyone, regardless of birth, background, or circumstance, can climb to any height. Work hard, study diligently, and the doors of opportunity will open.

This story is not entirely false. Education does provide real advantages. But the story is fatally incomplete, because it omits the most important variable of all: the quality of the school available to you is primarily a function of where you were born. And where you were born was not a choice you made.

In the United States, public school funding is tied primarily to local property taxes. This means that wealthy neighborhoods, with high property values and therefore high tax revenues, fund well-resourced schools with experienced teachers, robust facilities, and comprehensive extracurricular programs. Poor neighborhoods, with low property values, fund under-resourced schools with high teacher turnover, aging infrastructure, and stripped-down curricula. A child growing up two miles apart can inhabit educational worlds as different as different countries.

The Geography of Academic Achievement

The data on geographic educational inequality is staggering. In the United States, studies of standardized test scores reveal that neighborhood of residence predicts academic achievement more reliably than almost any other variable, including parental education level or individual student effort. The zip code a child is born into is, statistically speaking, one of the most powerful predictors of whether they will graduate high school, attend college, and what type of college they will attend.

This is not because children in poor neighborhoods are less intelligent or less ambitious. It is because they are proximate to fewer resources, less experienced teachers, smaller libraries, fewer advanced courses, and social environments where college attendance is less normalized. Proximity to educational quality, or its absence, compounds over years into dramatically different outcomes.

THE ZIP CODE EFFECT ON EDUCATION

Up to $11,000 per pupil

Annual per-student spending gap between the wealthiest and poorest school districts in many U.S. states. Children in poor districts attend school with a fraction of the resources available to children two towns over.

The same pattern holds globally. A child born in sub-Saharan Africa is proximate to educational systems with far fewer resources, lower-paid teachers, larger class sizes, and less reliable infrastructure than a child born in Finland or South Korea. The Finnish child does not study harder or possess superior genetics. They are simply proximate to a better-resourced system.

The University Clustering Effect

Elite universities do not distribute their graduates equally across the globe. They concentrate them. And the proximity of those graduates to power, opportunity, and networks creates compounding advantages that persist for generations.

Studies of the educational backgrounds of Fortune 500 CEOs, U.S. senators, Supreme Court justices, and top investment bankers consistently reveal extreme concentration in a handful of institutions. In any given year, a small cluster of elite universities (Harvard, Yale, Princeton, Stanford, MIT, Oxbridge) produce a wildly disproportionate share of leaders in virtually every field. Not because the education at these schools is so dramatically superior, but because proximity to the networks, opportunities, and credentialing these institutions confer is transformative.

This creates a deeply uncomfortable reality: the quality of educational institution a student can access is still primarily a function of proximity; specifically, proximity to the preparation and resources required to gain admission. Students who attended well-funded high schools, in affluent neighborhoods, with access to SAT tutors, college counselors, extracurricular programs, and parents who attended college themselves, arrive at the admissions process with enormous advantages. Those advantages are born of proximity to resources, not personal merit.

"The child who wins the Harvard admission lottery did not merely work

harder. They were born closer to the resources that make Harvard possible."

The Teacher Effect: Proximity to Excellence

Within any given school, proximity to an exceptional teacher is among the most powerful determinants of a student's trajectory. Research by economists Raj Chetty, John Friedman, and Jonah Rockoff found that having a high value-added teacher for even a single year produces measurable improvements in lifetime earnings for students. The assignment of a student to an exceptional rather than an average teacher can be the difference between a college trajectory and a non-college trajectory.

And how are students assigned to teachers? In most cases, by administrative processes that have nothing to do with student need or teacher-student compatibility. It is largely random. Which means whether you happen to be proximate to an excellent teacher at a formative moment in your education is substantially a matter of chance: the chance of being in the right class, in the right school, at the right time.

Mentorship and Proximity

Beyond formal education, proximity to mentors is a consistent predictor of career trajectory, innovation, and leadership emergence. Studies of Nobel Prize winners reveal that a disproportionate number of laureates were students or early-career researchers who worked directly, physically, alongside a previous Nobel winner. The transfer of knowledge, standards, ambition, and networks that occurs through close physical mentorship cannot be replicated by reading the same person's published work.

This pattern appears across domains. Jazz musicians who studied directly with great players. Athletes who trained under championship coaches. Entrepreneurs who apprenticed under successful founders. Writers who were edited by great editors. In each case, real, physical, ongoing proximity was the catalyst. What the apprentice received was not merely information that could have been conveyed in a book, but a modeling of standards, habits of mind, and access to networks that only close proximity makes possible.

The lesson for anyone invested in their own development is unambiguous: strategic proximity to exceptional people is more valuable than almost any credential, course, or program of self-study. Go where the best are. Seek proximity to excellence aggressively and deliberately, because proximity to excellence is itself a form of education that no institution can replicate.

"When the student is ready the teacher will appear."

"If I have seen further than others, it is by standing upon the shoulders of giants."

Chapter Three: Your Career Is a Geography Problem

"Luck is what happens when preparation meets opportunity."
Seneca, who forgot to mention that opportunity is where you are

The Industry Cluster Phenomenon

In 1998, the economist Michael Porter popularized the concept of industrial clusters: geographic concentrations of interconnected companies, suppliers, institutions, and associated industries in a particular field. His research, and the decades of work that followed it, established a foundational truth of economic geography: certain industries thrive in specific places because proximity between firms, talent, and institutions creates compounding advantages that cannot be easily replicated elsewhere.

Silicon Valley is the most famous example. The technology industry is globally distributed, yet a wildly disproportionate share of the world's most valuable technology companies, venture capital investment, and technological talent is concentrated within a roughly 50-mile strip of northern California. Hollywood dominates global film production. Wall Street dominates global finance. Nashville dominates country music. Detroit (and now a few other cities) dominates automotive manufacturing. The fashion industry clusters in Paris, Milan, New York, and London.

This is not coincidence. It is proximity dynamics at work. When exceptional talent, capital, suppliers, institutional knowledge, and informal networks all co-locate, they create a productive ecosystem whose whole is vastly greater than the sum of its parts. The startup founder in Silicon Valley has casual access to venture capitalists, experienced engineers, potential co-founders, and mentors who have built and sold companies before. Their counterpart in a smaller city may be equally talented and equally ambitious, but they are not proximate to those resources; that gap is frequently decisive.

THE INNOVATION GEOGRAPHY

Top 20 metro areas

account for roughly 90% of U.S. patent activity and venture capital investment, despite representing a small fraction of the country's geographic area and population.

A Manufacturing Cluster Up Close: BMW and the Upstate

The cluster phenomenon is not limited to knowledge industries or technology. One of the most instructive real-world illustrations sits in the Upstate of South Carolina, where BMW established its only American manufacturing plant in 1994. What followed is a textbook case of proximity dynamics in action.

BMW did not simply build a factory. It created a gravitational field. Within years, more than 500 South Carolina suppliers had oriented their operations around the plant, roughly 90 percent of them concentrated in the Upstate region. BMW prefers its most critical tier-one suppliers within what it internally describes as an imaginary circle of approximately 50 miles around the plant. Many are within a one to two hour drive. This is not sentiment or convenience. It is engineering.

The reason is Just-in-Time and Just-in-Sequence delivery: the lean manufacturing practice of receiving parts frequently, sometimes multiple times a day, precisely when they are needed on the line rather than warehousing them in advance. The entire system collapses without proximity. A supplier two time zones away cannot reliably deliver a custom interior panel four times a day. A supplier forty miles away can. Distance is not merely inconvenient in this model. It is structurally incompatible.

But proximity in the BMW cluster is more than logistics. It enables the kind of real-time collaboration that premium manufacturing requires: rapid response to quality issues, joint problem-solving when a design changes mid-production, shared workforce development programs, and the dense informal relationships between engineers and procurement teams that allow small problems to be solved before they become expensive ones. These benefits cannot be replicated by email or video call. They require people to be near enough to each other that a problem discovered at 7 a.m. can have an engineer on-site by 9 a.m.

The cluster also became self-reinforcing in the way all successful proximity ecosystems do. Once BMW was established, other major players followed, including Michelin, Bosch, and dozens of specialized component manufacturers. They came not only to serve BMW, but to participate in an ecosystem that now offers a concentrated skilled workforce, specialized training programs, shared infrastructure, and proximity to each other as sub-suppliers. The Inland Port in Greer, connected by rail to the Port of Charleston, completed the picture. The Upstate became one of the most productive manufacturing corridors in the American South not because of natural resources or historical accident, but because BMW's presence made it the most attractive point of proximity for everyone else in the supply chain.

BMW'S PROXIMITY CLUSTER

500+ suppliers

Support the BMW Spartanburg plant, with roughly 90% concentrated in the Upstate region of South Carolina — a self-reinforcing proximity ecosystem that supports tens of thousands of jobs beyond BMW's direct workforce.

The lesson extends far beyond automotive manufacturing. Every major industry creates its own version of this dynamic. The BMW example is simply unusually legible because the radius is quantified, the supply chain is documented, and the transformation of an entire region is visible on a map. The principle is universal: wherever one anchor institution of sufficient scale locates itself, it bends the proximity decisions of everyone connected to it. Your business, your career, your suppliers, your talent pool, and your competitive set all begin to organize around that gravitational center. Location is not merely a real estate decision. It is a strategic one that shapes every relationship your organization will ever have.

The Hidden Job Market and Proximity

Economists and career researchers have long documented what is called the hidden job market, referring to the large proportion of jobs that are filled without ever being publicly advertised. Estimates suggest that between 70 and 80 percent of professional positions are filled through personal connections and internal referrals rather than through open competition.

What drives access to those connections? Proximity. The colleague you have lunch with regularly. The classmate you bump into at the alumni event. The neighbor who works in the industry you are trying to break into. The acquaintance you see at the professional association meeting. These relationships, which are built and maintained through physical proximity and repeated contact, are the primary channels through which job opportunities actually flow.

This means that someone who has lived and worked in a major professional hub for a decade has built a network of proximity-based connections that someone entering that market from outside simply cannot match, regardless of their talent, credential, or effort. The person who is already proximate to the opportunity is almost always at an advantage over the person who is not.

"Most great jobs are never advertised. They are whispered to the person standing nearby."

The Commute and Performance

Proximity affects not just whether you get the job, but how well you perform once you have it. Research on commuting reveals that longer commutes are associated with reduced job satisfaction, higher stress, worse physical health, and lower productivity, independent of income level, job type, or individual characteristics. The simple physical distance between where you sleep and where you work has measurable effects on your wellbeing and performance.

Studies of academic researchers found that scientists who shared physical lab space produced significantly more collaborative papers, more cited research, and more breakthrough findings than scientists who were geographically separated, even when controlling for quality of institution, individual skill, and communication technology. The proximity of colleagues, including the ability to have a spontaneous conversation in the hallway, to share a meal, to see each other's work naturally; all of this produces collaborative benefits that no amount of email, video conferencing, or intentional remote coordination can fully replicate.

The Remote Work Test

The COVID-19 pandemic provided the largest natural experiment in the history of remote work. Millions of knowledge workers who had previously worked in offices were suddenly distributed. The productivity results were mixed but instructive. Workers who lived alone in small apartments in expensive cities suffered disproportionately. Workers who had home environments conducive to focus and who maintained regular social proximity with colleagues, even through digital means, fared better.

But the most instructive finding came from the years that followed. As companies assessed outcomes, a consistent pattern emerged: remote workers were less likely to be promoted. They were less likely to be assigned high-visibility projects. They were less likely to receive informal coaching and mentorship from senior leaders. They were, in short, disadvantaged by their absence of physical proximity to power.

Careers are not built purely on performance. They are built on visibility, relationship, and the accumulation of informal trust; all of which are primarily products of proximity. The hardest-working person in the building still has an advantage over the equally capable person working from home, because physical presence creates opportunities for visibility and connection that remote presence cannot fully replicate.

The Founding Team and Co-Location

Research on startup success consistently identifies team quality as the single most important predictor of venture outcomes. And what drives the formation of high-quality founding teams? Proximity. The world's most successful startups disproportionately began as teams of people who already knew each other: classmates from the same university cohort, former colleagues at the same company, members of the same professional community. Physical proximity preceded collaboration in every case.

Google was founded by two Stanford PhD students who shared an advisor. Apple began with two friends from the same neighborhood who shared an electronics obsession. Microsoft was founded by two childhood friends from Seattle. Facebook began in a Harvard dormitory. These are not coincidences. They are illustrations of a principle: trust, complementarity, and shared vision are the ingredients of great co-founding teams, and they are most easily forged by proximity.

Chapter Four: Your Health Is Your Address

"The most powerful determinant of your health is the environment in which you live, work, and age."
World Health Organization

The Social Determinants of Health

Public health researchers have known for decades what most individuals have not internalized: your health outcomes are more strongly determined by where you live than by your personal health decisions. What doctors call the social determinants of health (income, education, housing quality, neighborhood safety, access to nutritious food, air quality, water quality, and social connectedness) are all fundamentally geographic variables. They are things that your location determines, not things that your willpower determines.

The United States provides one of the starkest illustrations of this principle. The average life expectancy at birth in the wealthiest county in America exceeds the average life expectancy in the poorest county by more than twenty years. Twenty years of life, determined primarily by zip code. Not by genetics. Not by personal choices about diet and exercise. By geography.

LIFE EXPECTANCY AND ZIP CODE

20+ year gap

Between the wealthiest and poorest U.S. counties in average life expectancy. A child born into poverty may statistically lose two decades of life simply due to their geographic starting point.

Food Deserts and Proximity to Nutrition

What you eat, and therefore your metabolic health, your weight, and your risk of diabetes and heart disease, is powerfully shaped by what food is physically accessible to you. The concept of the food desert describes geographic areas where access to fresh, affordable, nutritious food is severely limited, typically because supermarkets and grocery stores are absent, and fast food and convenience stores dominate.

Food deserts disproportionately exist in low-income urban and rural communities. Residents of these communities face a simple arithmetic of proximity: a salad requires a twenty-minute bus ride, while a fast food meal is a three-minute walk. For working families with limited time and limited transportation, this proximity differential is decisive. The diet that results is not primarily a product of poor choices. It is a product of poor proximity.

Conversely, residents of affluent neighborhoods are proximate to multiple competing grocery chains, farmers markets, health food stores, and restaurants with nutritious options. Their diet advantages are not primarily a function of superior knowledge about nutrition or greater willpower. They are a function of what is near them.

The Disease Geography

Certain diseases cluster geographically with stunning precision. The stroke belt of the American South, where rates of cardiovascular disease and stroke are dramatically elevated compared to national averages, reflects a complex interaction of dietary traditions, healthcare access, environmental factors, and poverty; all of which are geographic variables. Cancer rates vary by county in ways that track industrial pollution, agricultural chemical use, and environmental contamination.

Air quality, which varies enormously by geography and has profound effects on respiratory health, cardiovascular health, cognitive development in children, and longevity, is determined by your proximity to industrial facilities, high-traffic roads, power plants, and wildfires. You did not choose to be downwind of a coal plant or to live adjacent to a highway interchange. But your proximity to those environmental hazards is shaping your lungs, your heart, and your brain.

Infectious disease is the most visceral example of proximity's power over health. Epidemics spread along networks of physical contact. The probability of contracting an infectious disease is directly proportional to your proximity to infected individuals, contaminated water, disease vectors, and the conditions that enable pathogen transmission. The Black Death, cholera, influenza, tuberculosis, and COVID-19: each pandemic in human history has been, at its core, a story of proximity.

Healthcare Access: Proximity to Cure

Geographic circumstances determine not only your likelihood of becoming ill but also your access to the care that might save you. The geographic distribution of healthcare resources in most countries is highly unequal. Specialty physicians, advanced diagnostic equipment, clinical trials, and cutting-edge treatment centers concentrate in major urban centers. Rural communities often have access only to general practitioners, with the nearest specialist hospital hours away.

The consequences of this proximity gap are measured in lives. Studies of heart attack patients consistently show that survival rates are significantly higher in urban areas with rapid access to catheterization labs than in rural areas where transfer times are longer. Cancer patients who live close to National Cancer Institute-designated comprehensive cancer centers receive more guideline-concordant care and have better survival outcomes than those who do not. The treatment you receive, and indeed whether it saves your life, is significantly determined by your proximity to the facilities that provide it.

The Social Proximity of Health Behaviors

Health behaviors are socially contagious. A landmark study by Nicholas Christakis and James Fowler, published in the New England Journal of Medicine, demonstrated that obesity spreads through social networks in patterns that resemble infectious disease transmission. If your close friend becomes obese, your probability of becoming obese increases by approximately 57 percent, even controlling for shared environmental factors. The same patterns have been documented for smoking, alcohol use, exercise habits, sleep duration, and mental health outcomes.

This social contagion occurs because health behaviors are normalized, modeled, and reinforced by the people physically around us. If everyone in your immediate social environment exercises regularly, you are exposed to a constant modeling of that behavior, to social accountability, to invitations to join fitness activities, and to a social norm that makes exercise the expected behavior. If everyone around you is sedentary, the opposite forces apply.

"You are the average of the 5 people you associate with most."

"You are the average of the five people you spend the most time with; not just in ambition, but in waistline, longevity, and lung capacity."

Mental health follows the same geographic and social patterns. Access to mental health services, the stigma or normalization of seeking help, and the prevalence of mental health resources are all geographically distributed. Rates of suicide, depression, and anxiety vary substantially by region, by urban versus rural residence, and by the social characteristics of communities. The mental health epidemic in rural America, driven partly by social isolation, partly by proximity to economic despair, and partly by the absence of mental health resources, is a proximity crisis as much as a clinical one.

Chapter Five: Born Rich, Born Poor. The Zip Code of Wealth

"In America, where you grow up has a bigger effect on your economic mobility than almost anywhere else in the developed world."
Raj Chetty, Harvard economist

The Geography of Opportunity

The American Dream holds that anyone, regardless of the circumstances of their birth, can achieve economic success through effort, intelligence, and perseverance. It is one of the most powerful national myths ever constructed. And it is, in significant part, a geographic fiction.

Raj Chetty and his colleagues at Harvard's Opportunity Insights project have produced what is arguably the most comprehensive study of economic mobility in American history. Their findings are startling: the probability that a child born into the bottom income quintile will reach the top income quintile as an adult varies enormously by county of birth. A child born in certain counties has a roughly one-in-twelve chance of escaping poverty. A child born in other counties has roughly a one-in-two chance. The variation is not explained primarily by differences in individual characteristics; it is explained primarily by geography.

ECONOMIC MOBILITY BY GEOGRAPHY

5x difference

In the probability of escaping poverty, depending on the county a child grows up in. Same country, same national opportunity rhetoric; radically different proximity to economic ladders.

The Mechanisms of Geographic Wealth Transmission

How does geography translate into wealth outcomes? The mechanisms are multiple and intertwining. First, as we have discussed, the quality of schools available to a child is geographically determined. Better schools produce better educational outcomes, which produce better career outcomes, which produce better income outcomes. The link from zip code to school to wealth is among the most well-documented causal chains in social science.

Second, the social networks available to a young person are geographically bounded. Your social capital, that is, who you know, is determined significantly by where you grew up, where you went to school, and where you work. Social capital is among the most powerful determinants of economic opportunity: it is what gives you access to job referrals, business introductions, investment capital, and the informal mentorship that accelerates careers. Growing up in a poor community means growing up in a social network that, on average, has less access to economic resources and fewer connections to the levers of opportunity.

Third, wealth itself concentrates geographically in ways that create feedback loops. High-value industries cluster in specific cities, driving up wages, housing values, and tax revenues in those places, which fund better services, attract more talent, and further accelerate the concentration of opportunity. The cities that are already rich get richer. The regions that are poor fall further behind. Geographic wealth divergence is not a natural law, but under current policy frameworks in most countries, it is a persistent and intensifying reality.

The Homeownership Geography

For most Americans, homeownership represents the primary vehicle of wealth accumulation. The value of a home is determined almost entirely by its location: its proximity to good schools, safe neighborhoods, employment centers, and amenity-rich communities. Two otherwise identical homes, built with the same materials, the same square footage, the same finishes, can differ in value by hundreds of thousands of dollars based solely on their geographic location.

This means that families who purchased homes in appreciating markets decades ago have accumulated wealth not primarily through their own efforts, but through the accident of geographic proximity to economic growth. Families who were historically excluded from homeownership in appreciating markets, through discriminatory practices like redlining, which explicitly denied mortgage credit to residents of predominantly Black neighborhoods, were robbed not just of housing, but of the primary wealth-building mechanism available to middle-class Americans, for reasons that were entirely geographic.

The Global Wealth Geography

Zoom out to the global scale, and the proximity story of wealth becomes even more dramatic. The average income in the ten wealthiest countries on Earth is roughly 50 to 100 times the average income in the ten poorest countries. The variation in per-capita economic output between nations dwarfs any other variable in predicting an individual's lifetime economic trajectory.

A person of average intelligence and average ambition, born in Norway or Switzerland, will almost certainly live a materially more prosperous life than a person of exceptional intelligence and extraordinary ambition born in Chad or the Central African Republic. Not because of character, not because of culture, not because of some inherent quality of the people; but because of their proximity to functioning institutions, to global trade networks, to political stability, to capital markets, and to the accumulated infrastructure of economic development.

This is perhaps the most uncomfortable implication of the proximity thesis: the accident of national birth is the single greatest determinant of an individual's lifetime economic prospects. We celebrate the self-made billionaire while ignoring that the same person, born in a different country, would almost certainly not be a billionaire, and might struggle to find clean drinking water.

"The most consequential lottery you ever won or lost was where you were born. You did not purchase a ticket."

The American Lottery: The Most Valuable Ticket You Never Bought

Among the great proximity lotteries of human history, being born in the United States of America stands in a category of its own. It is not the only winning ticket, but for the past century it has arguably been the most valuable one in circulation, and the vast majority of people who hold it have never paused to consider what it is actually worth.

To be born American is to arrive, without effort or merit, in proximity to a concentration of institutional, economic, legal, and cultural advantages that no other single nation on Earth currently replicates in full. The American-born person did not earn access to the world's largest economy, the world's reserve currency, the world's most extensive network of research universities, the world's deepest capital markets, the rule of law, the right to vote, freedom of speech and assembly, and the ability to move freely within a continental nation of 330 million people offering an almost incomprehensible diversity of economic opportunity. They simply arrived there. And that arrival, that single geographic accident of birth, changed everything about the material range of what their life could become.

THE AMERICAN BIRTH PREMIUM

~$77,000 per capita GDP

The United States GDP per capita versus a global average of roughly $13,000 and a median of under $8,000 — meaning the average American is born into an economy more than five times wealthier than the world average, before making a single personal choice.

Consider what American birth proximity actually provides. It provides proximity to the dollar: the global reserve currency, which means that American savings, investments, and earnings are denominated in an asset the entire world wants to hold. It provides proximity to the most liquid capital markets on Earth, meaning that an American with an idea can access venture capital, angel investment, small business loans, and public markets at a scale and speed unavailable to entrepreneurs in most other countries. It provides proximity to the legal infrastructure of contract enforcement, property rights, and intellectual property protection that makes sustained economic activity possible. It provides proximity to the National Institutes of Health, the FDA, the CDC, and the most advanced medical research apparatus in the world. And it provides proximity to a consumer market so vast and so affluent that succeeding within it alone can make you wealthy beyond the imagining of most of the world's population.

Then there is the cultural and linguistic proximity. To be born American is to be born a native speaker of English, the de facto global language of commerce, science, technology, and diplomacy. This is not a minor advantage. It means that the American entrepreneur, scientist, researcher, or professional operates in their native tongue within the language that dominates every global arena that matters economically. Their counterpart in Vietnam or Ethiopia or Bolivia must first overcome the barrier of operating in a second or third language before they can even access the same playing field.

To be born American is also to be born proximate to failure tolerance. The United States has, over its history, developed a cultural and legal infrastructure that is unusually forgiving of entrepreneurial failure. Bankruptcy laws allow individuals to reset. Social norms around failed ventures treat them as learning experiences rather than permanent stigmas. The result is a concentration of serial entrepreneurs, second-act innovators, and risk-takers who would not exist in the same numbers in cultures where a single failure carries permanent social and economic consequences. This proximity to a failure-tolerant ecosystem is itself a form of economic proximity that generates disproportionate innovation.

"The immigrant who crosses an ocean to reach America understands its value more clearly than most Americans do, because they can compare it to what they left behind."

Nobody understands the American proximity lottery more clearly than those who were not born into it and had to earn their way in. The naturalized citizen who grew up in a country without functioning courts, without reliable currency, without the freedom to start a business, without the right to vote, and then arrives in the United States often becomes its most articulate defender, not because of sentiment, but because they have a comparison point that the native-born American lacks. They know, viscerally and precisely, what the difference is worth. They have priced the lottery ticket because they have seen the alternative.

This is not an argument that America is without flaw, without injustice, or without profound inequalities of its own. The previous sections of this chapter have documented those inequalities in considerable detail. A Black child born in a poor neighborhood of Chicago and a white child born in an affluent suburb of Boston are both American, yet their proximity environments within America differ dramatically. The American lottery distributes its winnings very unevenly. But the external comparison is still staggering: even the American who grows up in poverty has access to free public education, emergency medical care, a legal system with enforceable rights, and the freedom of movement to seek better opportunities elsewhere in the country. These are not guaranteed anywhere. They are proximity advantages that billions of people on this planet do not have.

The most clarifying thought experiment is this: take a person of any background, any temperament, any level of intelligence and ambition, and ask what range of outcomes their life can reach if they are born in the United States versus if they are born in North Korea, or Yemen, or the Democratic Republic of Congo. The individual is identical. The proximity environment is entirely different. The range of possible lives diverges so dramatically that the comparison almost cannot be made in the same units. That divergence is the proximity lottery, and America, for all its contradictions, remains one of the most powerful winning tickets it is possible to hold.

The practical implication of this is one that comfortable Americans rarely dwell on: the baseline of prosperity, safety, and opportunity that many Americans experience as ordinary, as the floor of a normal life, is for most of the world an unattainable ceiling. The American who feels frustrated by their station in life, who feels that they have not achieved what they deserved, is almost always comparing themselves upward, to others within America. They are rarely comparing themselves outward, to the seven billion human beings who do not share their proximity to the institutional, economic, and legal infrastructure they inherited at birth. That outward comparison does not diminish legitimate frustrations about inequality within America. But it does provide essential context for understanding just how consequential the accident of American birth truly is.

Chapter Six: The Faith of Geography. Religion and Belief

"If you were born in Saudi Arabia, you would almost certainly be Muslim. If you were born in Mississippi, you would likely be Baptist. If you were born in Tibet, you might be Buddhist. Geography is theology."
Anonymous sociologist

The Geographic Distribution of Faith

There are currently an estimated 4,200 distinct religions practiced on Earth, ranging from the world's largest faith traditions (Christianity, Islam, Hinduism, Buddhism, Judaism) to thousands of smaller indigenous spiritual traditions. These faiths make mutually exclusive claims about the nature of reality, the existence and character of God or gods, the path to salvation or liberation, and the moral requirements of a good life.

Here is the empirical fact that deserves our sustained attention: which of these religious traditions a person embraces is predicted with extraordinary accuracy by a single variable: where they were born. A child born in Iran has a roughly 98 percent probability of being raised Muslim. A child born in Mexico has a roughly 83 percent probability of being raised Catholic. A child born in Thailand has a roughly 95 percent probability of being raised Buddhist. A child born in Israel is overwhelmingly likely to be raised Jewish. A child born in India is overwhelmingly likely to be raised Hindu.

These are not marginal statistical tendencies. They are near-deterministic relationships. The faith you hold most deeply, including the beliefs you may feel are the product of personal revelation, spiritual search, and genuine conviction, is, in the vast majority of cases, the direct inheritance of your geographic and familial proximity to a particular tradition.

RELIGION BY GEOGRAPHY

~90%+ correlation

Between place of birth and religious identity in most countries. The faith you consider your deepest personal truth is overwhelmingly likely to be the faith of your neighborhood.

The Transmission Mechanism

How does geographic proximity transmit religious identity? The mechanisms are numerous and deeply embedded in human social life. Children are raised in the religious traditions of their parents, who were themselves raised in the traditions of their parents, in a continuous chain of cultural transmission that runs through specific geographic communities. Religious institutions (churches, mosques, synagogues, temples, monasteries) are physically located in specific places and serve the surrounding population. Religious schools, rituals, festivals, and social networks are locally organized and locally reinforced.

The result is that religious belief is not primarily the product of individual rational inquiry into which metaphysical framework best accounts for human experience. It is primarily the product of proximity: proximity to a tradition's practitioners, institutions, texts, and cultural forms, experienced from the earliest age, during the most formative years of cognitive and identity development.

This does not make religious belief less genuine or less meaningful. The person who believes deeply in the tradition they were born into is not being insincere. They are expressing a conviction that has been shaped by years of genuine experience within that tradition. But intellectual honesty requires acknowledging that the same person, born in a different place, would almost certainly hold a different set of equally genuine convictions.

Secularism as a Geographic Phenomenon

Even the absence of religious belief, including secularism, atheism, and religious non-affiliation, follows geographic patterns. The highly secularized societies of northern and western Europe, particularly in Scandinavia, reflect not some inherent European rationality, but a specific historical trajectory of Enlightenment thought, institutional church reform, and social policy that created communities where non-belief became normalized and socially permissible. The high rates of religious non-affiliation in urban areas of the United States compared to rural areas reflects similar proximity dynamics: urban density exposes individuals to diverse viewpoints, challenges parochial certainties, and normalizes a range of belief and non-belief.

In other words, if you are an atheist reading this book, your atheism, like the religious believer's faith, is significantly a product of your proximity to ideas, communities, and social environments that made atheism thinkable, expressible, and socially sustainable. You did not arrive at your worldview in a vacuum.

Political and Moral Beliefs: The Same Geography

What applies to religious belief applies with equal force to political ideology and moral conviction. Research by social psychologist Jonathan Haidt and others has documented that political beliefs, while partly rooted in individual personality traits, are powerfully shaped by geographic and social context. Communities with high density, high diversity, high exposure to global trade and culture, and high concentrations of university-educated residents tend toward political liberalism. Communities that are more rural, more economically homogeneous, more culturally stable, and more socially tight-knit tend toward political conservatism.

These are not primarily differences in reasoning ability or moral seriousness. They are differences in proximity to the circumstances that shape worldview. The person who has lived their entire life in a small, homogeneous rural community will have very different priors about the nature of society, the trustworthiness of strangers, the importance of tradition, and the risks of rapid change than the person who has lived in a diverse global city. Both perspectives reflect genuine experience. Both are proximity-shaped.

"Your deepest beliefs about God, justice, morality, and politics were not discovered through reason alone. They were absorbed from the air of the place you grew up."

Chapter Seven: You Speak Because of Where You Are

"Language is not merely a tool for communication. It is the architecture of thought. You did not choose its blueprint."
Ludwig Wittgenstein, adapted

The Language Lottery

There are approximately 7,000 languages spoken on Earth today. Each one is not merely a different set of labels for the same underlying reality. Languages differ in their phonological systems, their grammatical structures, their categorization of time and space, their color vocabularies, their capacity to express certain emotional or philosophical distinctions. Research in the psychology of language, particularly the work of Benjamin Lee Whorf though interpreted with appropriate nuance, suggests that the language you think in shapes, at least to some degree, the contours of your thought.

You speak the language you speak, and think the thoughts that language enables, because of where you were born. Not because you evaluated 7,000 options and selected the most expressive, the most logical, or the most beautiful. You speak Mandarin or Arabic or Spanish or English or Swahili because you were born proximate to speakers of that language. Your linguistic world, which is also your cognitive and communicative world, was assigned to you by geography.

This has profound and underappreciated consequences. The language you speak determines what communities you can participate in, what literature you can access in its original form, what global economic opportunities are open to you, what scientific and cultural production you can engage with directly. English speakers, by accident of birth, are proximate to the dominant language of global commerce, science, and technology. This is not a function of the English language's inherent superiority; it is a function of the historical and economic forces that made English globally dominant, which are themselves geographic and political forces.

Accent and Social Proximity

Even within a single language, accent and dialect, both products of geographic proximity to specific speech communities, carry enormous social weight. Research on accent discrimination consistently shows that speakers of stigmatized regional or ethnic accents face discrimination in hiring, in judicial proceedings, in medical care, and in social interactions. The Received Pronunciation of British English, the General American accent of U.S. broadcast media, and the Parisian French of formal education are not linguistically superior to regional variants. They carry prestige because of their proximity to power; they were the accents of the socially dominant communities.

A person born in Appalachia, the Mississippi Delta, or the East End of London carries their geographic origin in their voice. That accent opens some doors and closes others, creating a form of identity that is inescapably tied to place.

Cultural Taste and Geographic Formation

The music you love, the food you crave, the aesthetic preferences you carry, the jokes you find funny, the films that move you: none of these are simply products of individual taste. They are products of cultural proximity. You were exposed, repeatedly and from early childhood, to the cultural production of your geographic community. That exposure shaped neural pathways of preference and association that feel personal and intrinsic but are, in large measure, artifacts of place.

This is why nostalgia is so powerfully tied to location. The smell of a particular food, the sound of a particular kind of music, the sight of a particular landscape: all of these trigger intense emotional responses precisely because they are encoded as markers of the proximate community that formed you. Your identity is, in this deep sense, a geographic identity.

The globalization of culture through digital media has partially disrupted this pattern, creating the possibility of cultural communities that are distributed across geography. Someone in rural Kansas can now be deeply embedded in Korean pop culture, or Japanese anime, or West African music. Digital proximity is creating new forms of cultural community that transcend physical location. But the power of local cultural proximity, including the food, the music, the humor, and the social rituals of the place where you grew up, remains extraordinarily powerful in shaping individual identity.

Chapter Eight: The Crime of Geography

"Most people who commit crimes are not bad people. They are people in bad places."
David Kennedy, criminologist

The Geography of Crime

Criminologists have documented for decades what police officers have always known intuitively: crime is not randomly distributed. It clusters. It concentrates in specific places (specific blocks, specific intersections, specific buildings) with a precision that defies any explanation rooted purely in individual pathology or personal moral failure.

The concept of crime hot spots, referring to geographic locations with disproportionately high rates of criminal activity, is among the most robust findings in criminology. Research by Lawrence Sherman and his colleagues established that in most cities, roughly 50 percent of all crime occurs in just 3 to 5 percent of all geographic locations. Crime is not primarily a people problem. It is a place problem.

This has radical implications for how we understand individual criminal behavior. The person who commits a crime is not simply enacting an internal moral deficiency. They are, in most cases, responding to the confluence of environmental factors that their geographic location has placed them in proximity to: concentrated poverty, absence of legitimate economic opportunity, exposure to criminal role models, presence of criminal networks and markets, absence of institutional protective factors like effective policing, stable employment, and quality education.

CRIME CONCENTRATION

~3-5% of locations

Account for roughly 50% of all crime in most U.S. cities. Crime is not a people problem uniformly distributed; it is a place problem tightly concentrated.

Proximity to Violence and Developmental Harm

Growing up in proximity to violence, whether witnessed in the home, in the street, or in the school, has profound and well-documented effects on child development. Exposure to violence activates the stress response system, disrupts healthy neural development, impairs executive function and impulse control, and increases the probability of behavioral problems, academic failure, and eventual criminal involvement. Proximity to violence is not merely an unpleasant childhood experience. It is a developmental injury.

The child who grows up in a neighborhood where gun violence is routine is not making a lifestyle choice. They are being subjected to an environmental exposure that physiologically and psychologically shapes who they become. The behavioral and cognitive effects of that exposure will follow them for years, even decades, regardless of how far they eventually move from the neighborhood that caused the damage.

The Justice Geography

Proximity shapes not just who commits crime but who is prosecuted for it, convicted of it, and imprisoned for it. The geographic distribution of policing resources means that crime in high-poverty, high-police-presence neighborhoods is detected and prosecuted at far higher rates than equivalent crime in wealthy, low-police-presence neighborhoods. The same drug possession offense, committed with identical frequency across social classes, results in dramatically different criminal justice outcomes depending on the geography of the offense, which is largely a function of the race and class of the perpetrator's neighborhood.

The United States imprisons more of its citizens than any other nation on Earth, and the geography of incarceration is not random. The majority of people imprisoned come from a small number of neighborhoods in a small number of cities. The economic disruption of mass incarceration, including removing breadwinners, saddling individuals with criminal records that limit employment, and disrupting community social structures, is concentrated geographically, creating compounding disadvantage in the places already most vulnerable.

"Prison is, among other things, a geographic sorting mechanism; it concentrates punishment in the places that were already most punished."

Chapter Nine: The Latitude of Happiness

"Happiness is not found. It is inherited from your surroundings."
Anonymous

The Geography of Wellbeing

The field of happiness research, encompassing positive psychology, wellbeing science, and hedonic economics, has generated an enormous literature on the determinants of subjective life satisfaction. Much of this literature has focused on individual-level variables: genetics, personality, relationship status, income, physical health, and sense of meaning and purpose. These variables matter. But a growing body of research reveals that geography, specifically where you live, is a powerful and underappreciated predictor of happiness, independent of these individual factors.

The World Happiness Report, published annually by the United Nations Sustainable Development Solutions Network, reveals enormous variation in average national happiness levels that track, with remarkable consistency, geographic and institutional variables. The Scandinavian nations (Finland, Denmark, Norway, Sweden) perennially top the rankings. Sub-Saharan African nations perennially appear at the bottom. These differences are not primarily genetic, and they are not primarily explained by individual differences in personality or life philosophy. They are explained by geographic and institutional variables: income equality, social trust, government effectiveness, social support systems, and freedom from corruption.

Social Contagion of Happiness

Nicholas Christakis and James Fowler, whose work we encountered in the health chapter, applied the same social network analysis to happiness that they had applied to obesity. Their findings, published in the British Medical Journal, were striking: happiness is contagious in social networks. Having a happy friend within a mile of you increases the probability of your own happiness by approximately 25 percent. The effect diminishes with geographic distance and with social network distance; it is weaker for friends who live farther away, and weaker for more socially distant connections.

Conversely, having unhappy people in your immediate social and geographic environment is associated with reduced personal happiness. The emotional climate of your proximate community, including the baseline mood, the level of trust, the prevalence of stress and anxiety, and the presence or absence of social support, creates a kind of emotional weather that envelops you and significantly influences your own psychological state.

SOCIAL PROXIMITY AND HAPPINESS

+25% likelihood

Of being happy if a close friend within one mile of you is happy. Emotional wellbeing spreads through geographic social networks like a benign contagion.

Urban Versus Rural Wellbeing

The relationship between urbanization and happiness is complex and has been much debated. Studies find that cities offer certain proximity advantages: greater access to cultural amenities, social diversity, economic opportunity, and the stimulating variety of urban life. But they also impose proximity costs: greater noise, crowding, commuting stress, social anonymity, and often less access to green space and natural environments.

Research consistently finds that proximity to green space (parks, forests, bodies of water, natural landscapes) is associated with improved mental health, reduced stress, lower rates of depression, and higher life satisfaction. People who live within walking distance of parks or natural areas report significantly higher wellbeing than those who do not, controlling for income and other variables. Your proximity to nature is not a luxury amenity; it is a determinant of psychological health.

The social isolation of rural environments, combined with fewer economic opportunities and more limited access to mental health services, is associated with elevated rates of depression, anxiety, and suicide in many rural communities. But the specific forms of community connection available in tight-knit rural communities, such as the social support of neighbors who have known each other for generations and the sense of belonging to a place, can provide a form of wellbeing that the anonymous freedom of urban life does not.

Sense of Place and Identity

Psychologists studying place attachment, defined as the emotional and psychological bonds that individuals form with specific geographic locations, have found that a sense of belonging to a place is a significant contributor to wellbeing. People who feel deeply rooted in a community, who have long-term relationships with neighbors, who participate in local institutions, and who identify with the history and character of a place, report higher levels of meaning and life satisfaction than those who feel geographically rootless.

This creates a tension in a highly mobile modern world. Geographic mobility, defined as the willingness to move to where opportunity exists, is often a rational economic strategy. But it comes with a wellbeing cost: the disruption of place-based social networks, the loss of community belonging, the psychological toll of starting over in a new environment. Understanding this tension is essential for making conscious choices about when to move to expand proximity to opportunity, and when to stay to protect proximity to community and belonging.

Chapter Ten: You Vote Like Your Neighbors

"Show me where someone lives, and I will tell you how they vote with near-perfect accuracy."
Every political data scientist

The Spatial Sort of Political America

In the contemporary United States, there is perhaps no better illustration of proximity as a determinant of belief and behavior than the geography of political identity. The political sorting of America by geography has accelerated dramatically in recent decades, producing a nation where where you live is one of the most reliable predictors of how you vote, what media you consume, what moral values you prioritize, and what political reality you inhabit.

The urban-rural divide in American politics is not simply a divide between different preferences; it is a divide between different proximity environments that generate genuinely different social experiences, economic circumstances, and therefore genuinely different political perspectives. The urban resident who supports robust immigration and celebrates demographic diversity has, in most cases, daily proximity to immigrants and diverse communities, and their political position reflects their actual lived experience. The rural resident who feels anxious about immigration and demographic change has, in many cases, had less proximate experience with the diversity they fear. Both positions reflect their proximity environments, not simply their character.

The Echo Chamber: Proximity to Like-Mindedness

The geographic sorting of America by political identity has created what political scientists call ideological segregation: the increasing tendency of Americans to live in communities where nearly everyone agrees with them politically. This proximity to like-mindedness has profound effects on political belief. Research consistently shows that living in a politically homogeneous community strengthens partisan identity, increases political polarization, and reduces empathy for opposing viewpoints.

When you are surrounded by people who share your political assumptions, who use the same political language, consume the same media, and validate the same political judgments, your views feel not like opinions but like obvious facts. The partisan who lives in a 90-percent-Democrat or 90-percent-Republican neighborhood cannot easily imagine how a reasonable person could disagree with their political worldview, because they are rarely proximate to such people.

This proximity-driven political radicalization is not primarily a failure of individual reason. It is a predictable consequence of ideological geographic sorting. The solution is greater geographic integration of people with different political perspectives; this is a proximity intervention, not merely a call for open-mindedness.

"Political polarization is not fundamentally a media problem or a moral problem. It is a proximity problem; we have sorted ourselves into echo chambers of geography."

Global Political Geography

Internationally, the same pattern holds at every scale. Citizens of democratic countries have proximity to democratic institutions, civic norms, and the lived experience of political accountability that shapes their political expectations. Citizens of authoritarian states have proximity to entirely different political institutions and norms, which shapes entirely different political dispositions and tolerances.

The person who grows up in a functioning democracy develops intuitions about civic participation, institutional accountability, and political rights that feel obvious and natural, because they have been in daily proximity to a social and political environment that makes those values real and enforceable. The person who grows up under authoritarianism develops different intuitions; not because they are less intelligent or less worthy of freedom, but because they are proximate to different political realities.

This should make us humble about attributing political outcomes to culture, character, or the intrinsic values of particular peoples. Political culture is, in large measure, a product of the political institutions and social environments that populations have been in proximity to over time. Change the proximity environment, through institutional reform, international integration, or the simple experience of living in a different political system, and political culture can change within generations.

Chapter Eleven: The Genius of Place. Innovation and Opportunity

"Cities are the greatest invention of the human species, because they are the greatest amplifier of human proximity."
Edward Glaeser, economist

Why Cities Make Us Smarter

The economist Edward Glaeser has spent a career documenting one of the most striking facts in economic history: cities, despite their costs and difficulties, make people more productive, more innovative, more creative, and more prosperous than rural living. And the primary mechanism is proximity.

When talented, ambitious, knowledgeable people are concentrated in a small geographic area, they produce a superlinear explosion of ideas, innovations, and economic value. The density of human interaction in cities creates what economists call agglomeration effects: spillovers of knowledge, skill, and creativity that occur when diverse expertise is proximate. The Silicon Valley engineer who has lunch with a biologist and an economist, by accident of geographic co-location, may produce a business idea that none of the three could have generated alone.

Glaeser's research shows that doubling the population density of a city is associated with a roughly 15 percent increase in productivity per capita. Not because city people are inherently smarter or more capable, but because the density of their proximity produces more connections, more collaborations, more serendipitous encounters, and more rapid transmission of ideas. Cities are, in this sense, proximity amplifiers; they are machines for concentrating the productive benefits of human intellectual exchange.

The Death of Distance? Not Quite

The digital revolution was supposed to eliminate the advantages of geographic proximity. In the information age, the reasoning went, talent could be anywhere; software could be written in Bangalore or Lagos as effectively as in San Francisco, financial analysis in Warsaw as capably as in London. Geographic proximity would become irrelevant; the frictionless exchange of information would make it so.

This has not happened. Despite decades of communication technology that has made the exchange of information essentially costless regardless of geography, the economic and innovative advantages of geographic clusters have not diminished, and in some respects have intensified. Silicon Valley's dominance in technology has, if anything, strengthened in the digital age. Wall Street's dominance in global finance persists. The concentration of pharmaceutical innovation in a small number of cities with major research universities and established biotech clusters has, if anything, increased.

Why? Because the most valuable forms of knowledge are not codified; they are not the kind of information that can be sent in an email or conveyed in a Zoom call. They are tacit: the intuitions, judgment, relationships, and contextual understanding that are acquired through prolonged immersion in an environment where the relevant expertise is practiced and discussed daily. Tacit knowledge transfers through proximity, through apprenticeship, through shared experience, through the kind of informal conversation that happens when you are physically co-located with experts in a field. No digital technology has successfully replicated this mechanism.

INNOVATION GEOGRAPHY

Top 5 metro areas

Account for the majority of U.S. venture capital investment, patent activity, and tech startup formation. In the digital age, geography remains the dominant variable in innovation.

The Serendipity Premium

One of the most underappreciated mechanisms of proximity-driven innovation is serendipity: the unplanned, accidental encounter that produces unexpected insight. The history of scientific and technological innovation is littered with discoveries that occurred not through systematic search but through accidental proximity: Alexander Fleming noticing a contaminated petri dish that revealed penicillin. Watson and Crick's crucial conversation with a colleague about Rosalind Franklin's X-ray diffraction data. The chance meeting at a conference that sparks a multi-year collaboration. The hallway conversation that unlocks a problem being worked on in stubborn isolation for months.

And then there is the experience most readers of this book will recognize from their own lives: you have been wrestling with a complex problem for weeks or months. You have read everything available. You have consulted your usual sources. You have turned the question over so many times in your mind that you have stopped being able to see it clearly. And then, at a dinner party or a conference or a chance encounter at the coffee shop, you meet someone. The conversation turns, almost accidentally, to the problem you have been carrying. And within minutes, it becomes apparent that this person has either solved exactly that problem before, or knows someone who has, or brings a perspective from an entirely different domain that cracks the question open like a walnut.

In that moment, the feeling is often one of wonder. Of having been led somewhere. Some people call it divine intervention. Some call it the law of attraction. Some attribute it to the universe responding to their intentions. These are not unreasonable emotional responses to a genuinely striking experience. But they are the wrong explanation. And having the wrong explanation means you cannot reliably reproduce the experience.

"The universe did not send you that person. You went to the room where that person was. That is a crucial difference."

The right explanation is proximity math. Every time you place yourself in an environment that concentrates people who are working on difficult problems in your domain or adjacent domains, you increase the probability that one of them is carrying a solution to your current question. It is not mystical. It is combinatorics. If you are working on a problem in, say, supply chain optimization, and you attend a conference of three hundred supply chain professionals, you have placed yourself in proximity to three hundred people whose professional lives overlap substantially with yours. The probability that at least one of them has encountered your problem, or a close variant of it, is very high. The probability that a conversation will surface that overlap is proportional to how many conversations you have. None of this requires the universe to arrange anything. It only requires you to show up.

The sociologist Mark Granovetter identified a related phenomenon in his landmark research on what he called the strength of weak ties. His counterintuitive finding was that the most valuable information and opportunities tend to arrive not through your closest relationships, but through acquaintances and near-strangers, people who move in social circles adjacent to but not identical with your own. Your close friends and colleagues largely share your knowledge base. They know what you know, read what you read, and have been exposed to the same set of solutions you have already considered. The stranger at the conference, the acquaintance you rarely see, the person seated next to you at an industry dinner, these are the people most likely to bring genuinely new information, because they inhabit a different proximity environment from yours. Their knowledge is different from your knowledge precisely because they have been somewhere different.

THE WEAK TIES EFFECT

~83% of new job leads

In Granovetter's research, the large majority of valuable professional information and opportunities arrived through weak ties — acquaintances seen occasionally or rarely — not through close friends. The weaker the tie, the more likely it crosses into a different knowledge world.

This is why the experience of meeting exactly the right person at exactly the right moment happens more frequently to people who go to more things. It is not that they are cosmically favored. It is that they have a larger serendipity surface area. Every conference attended, every professional dinner accepted, every networking event endured, every coffee meeting that seemed like an unlikely use of time, each of these is an expansion of the probability field within which a useful collision can occur. The person who stays home, who manages their network digitally, who conserves their time and energy by declining invitations, is mathematically reducing their exposure to the serendipitous encounter. They are not being efficient. They are being invisible to chance.

There is a concept sometimes called luck surface area, the idea that luck is not purely random but is proportional to the number of people who know what you are working on and the number of environments in which you are actively present. Share your problem with more people, in more places, among more diverse crowds, and you increase the probability that the right person will hear it and recognize that they hold a relevant piece of the solution. The entrepreneur who talks about their startup problem at every dinner they attend is not being tiresome. They are running a distributed search operation, deploying human sensors across every room they enter, any one of which might trigger the connection they need.

The physical environment matters enormously to this dynamic. The serendipitous encounter is not merely possible in proximity-dense environments; it is structurally produced by them. Bell Labs, the legendary research facility that generated more transformative innovations per square foot than perhaps any institution in history, was famously designed by its directors to force accidental encounters. The building's long corridors required researchers from different disciplines to pass each other regularly. The cafeteria was a single space. The result was that a physicist working on transistors might find himself in daily proximity to a mathematician working on information theory, and from that daily proximity came the kind of cross-domain insight that produced the transistor, the laser, information theory, and the Unix operating system. Not by design, but by proximity.

The question, then, is not whether you believe in serendipity. Of course you should. The question is whether you understand its mechanism. If you believe it is divine, you will wait for it, grateful when it arrives and puzzled when it does not. If you understand it as proximity, you will engineer the conditions that make it more likely: going to more places, talking to more people across a wider range of domains, sharing your problems openly rather than hoarding them, and above all placing yourself physically in the environments where the relevant people are already concentrated. The universe is not conspiring to bring you answers. The room you walk into might be. Choose your rooms accordingly.

Serendipity is not random. It is a function of proximity: being in the right environment, around the right people, at the right moment. The dense, diverse, intellectually active environment of a major research university or a world-class innovation cluster generates serendipity at a rate that no intentionally designed process can match, because the most valuable creative connections cannot be anticipated in advance. They can only be enabled by proximity.

The Black Swan and the Proximity Premium

Nassim Nicholas Taleb, in The Black Swan: The Impact of the Highly Improbable, makes an argument that at first appears to be about randomness but is, at its core, an argument about proximity. Taleb distinguishes between what he calls Mediocristan, domains where outcomes are constrained and predictable, like height or physical strength, and Extremistan, domains where a single event can have an outcome wildly disproportionate to anything that came before it: wealth, reputation, scientific discovery, creative breakthrough, influence.

In Extremistan, Taleb argues, the most powerful strategy is not to predict which rare event will occur, since by definition you cannot, but to maximize your exposure to positive rare events while limiting your exposure to catastrophic negative ones. And his most concrete practical advice for achieving this? Move to, or position yourself in, the largest and most active hubs of human exchange you can access. Cities. Industry conferences. Research institutions. Innovation clusters. Anywhere that concentrates diverse, ambitious, well-connected people in sufficient density that the probability of a transformative unexpected encounter is materially higher than it would be in a smaller, quieter, more predictable setting.

Taleb calls these positive outlier events positive Black Swans, and he observes that they disproportionately occur to people who are in proximity to the conditions that make them possible: density, diversity, movement of ideas and capital, and the kind of productive chaos that organized environments suppress. The hermit waiting in a cabin for inspiration is not practicing patience. He is reducing his luck surface area to near zero. The person embedded in a dense, active, cross-disciplinary environment is not merely socializing. They are running a continuous probabilistic experiment in which the expected value of each new conversation is positive, even though no individual conversation can be predicted in advance.

"Position yourself where positive Black Swans can find you. They cannot reach a cabin in the woods."

This is the deepest argument for proximity as a life strategy. It is not merely that proximity gives you access to known opportunities, though it does. It is that proximity generates the conditions for opportunities that nobody could have anticipated, including you. The proximity premium, in Extremistan domains, is not linear. It is exponential. And the cities, institutions, and communities that concentrate human talent and restless ambition are not just pleasant places to be. They are the environments in which the outlier events that change lives and industries are most likely to be born.

The Digital Proximity Frontier

Online communities, remote work platforms, and digital social networks are creating new forms of proximity that transcend physical geography. A programmer in Lagos who is deeply embedded in an open-source software community, who interacts daily with the leading figures in the field, contributes to respected projects, and builds a reputation within that community, is experiencing a form of digital proximity to excellence and opportunity that was impossible twenty years ago.

This is genuinely new and genuinely important. For the first time in history, a motivated individual with internet access can position themselves in proximity to ideas, networks, and opportunities that were previously accessible only to those born in specific geographic locations. This does not eliminate the advantages of physical proximity; it supplements them. And it creates, for the first time, a path for individuals to overcome some of the proximity disadvantages of their physical location through deliberate cultivation of digital proximity.

But this path is narrow and demanding. It requires motivation, access to high-speed internet, English language proficiency (for most global knowledge communities), digital literacy, and the ability to sustain online engagement without the social reinforcement of physical community. The digital proximity revolution is real, but it has not yet democratized opportunity. It has created a new form of geographic-adjacent inequality, between those who can access and leverage digital proximity and those who cannot.

Chapter Twelve: The Proximity of Prejudice. Race, Identity, and Social Distance

"Fear of the stranger is proportional to distance from them."
Gordon Allport, paraphrased

Contact Theory and Proximity

In 1954, the social psychologist Gordon Allport published The Nature of Prejudice, one of the most influential works in the history of social psychology. In it, he advanced what became known as the contact hypothesis: that prejudice between groups decreases when members of those groups are brought into direct, equal-status, cooperative contact with one another.

Allport's hypothesis, which has been tested and refined in hundreds of studies across decades, is fundamentally a proximity thesis. Prejudice thrives on distance: on the absence of real, human contact between members of different groups. It relies on stereotypes and generalizations that can only be maintained when real individuals from the stigmatized group are not proximate enough to disrupt them. When people actually live near, work alongside, and build relationships with those who are different from themselves, prejudice systematically decreases; not in every case, not instantly, but as a robust empirical tendency.

The implications are significant. The areas of the United States with the highest levels of racial prejudice are, historically, not the areas with the highest levels of racial diversity and daily intergroup contact.

They are often the areas with the least. Prejudice flourishes in geographic isolation from its object.

Structural Segregation as Proximity Management

For much of American history, legal and social mechanisms explicitly managed the proximity between racial groups, ensuring that Black Americans and white Americans lived in separate neighborhoods, attended separate schools, worshipped in separate churches, and worked in separate industries. This was not merely a moral injustice. It was, in the framework of this book, a deliberate proximity intervention: a systematic effort to prevent the contact that Allport's hypothesis predicts would reduce prejudice and, over time, challenge racial hierarchy.

Residential segregation by race, which remains significant in most American metropolitan areas decades after the formal legal apparatus of segregation was dismantled, continues to limit the proximate contact between racial groups that might otherwise erode prejudice and build intergroup understanding. The neighborhood you grew up in, its racial composition, its economic character, its relationship to surrounding communities, shaped your intuitions, assumptions, and emotional responses to racial difference in ways you may not fully recognize.

The Proximity Solution

If prejudice is partly a proximity deficit, then its solution must involve proximity interventions. Integrated schools, integrated neighborhoods, diverse workplaces, and inclusive social institutions are not merely politically correct aspirations. They are, if Allport's contact hypothesis holds (and substantial evidence suggests it does), empirically effective mechanisms for reducing prejudice and building the cross-group social trust on which pluralistic societies depend.

This is why the geography of school integration matters so much. When children of different racial, ethnic, and economic backgrounds attend the same schools and participate in the same activities from an early age, they build proximity-based knowledge of each other; knowledge that disrupts stereotypes, builds empathy, and creates adult citizens who are more comfortable with and capable of functioning in diverse environments. The de-integration of American schools that has occurred in recent decades has proximity consequences that will be felt for generations.

Chapter Thirteen: Digital Proximity. The New Geography

"The internet didn't kill geography. It created a new one."
Unknown

From Physical to Digital Neighborhoods

For the majority of human history, proximity was exclusively physical. Your community was determined by the people who lived within walking distance, and later within riding or driving distance. The constraints of physical geography were the constraints of social life.

The emergence of digital communication networks (email, social media, forums, multiplayer gaming, streaming platforms, professional networks) has created a new form of community that is organized around interest, identity, and affiliation rather than physical location. For the first time, a teenager in rural Montana can be a genuine, active member of a community of astrophysics enthusiasts, competitive chess players, K-pop fans, or Rust programmers that spans the globe. The radius of potential community has expanded from a few miles to the entire connected world.

This is a genuine and profound expansion of human possibility. But it comes with new proximity dynamics that replicate some of the most troubling features of physical proximity while eliminating some of its most valuable ones.

The Algorithm as Proximity Architecture

In the physical world, proximity is determined by geography: by the accident of where you were born and where you choose to live. In the digital world, proximity is determined by algorithms; specifically, by the computational systems that decide which content, which people, and which communities appear in your feed, your search results, your recommended connections.

These algorithms, optimized primarily for engagement rather than truth, accuracy, or social wellbeing, tend to bring you into proximity with content and perspectives that reinforce your existing beliefs and emotional responses. This algorithmic proximity is a new and powerful form of the echo chamber effect; more pervasive than its geographic predecessor because it follows you everywhere you go and is updated in real time based on your responses.

The radicalization pathways documented in YouTube's recommendation algorithm, the filter bubbles of Facebook's news feed, and the polarizing dynamics of Twitter's outrage cycle are all proximity phenomena: they are the result of an algorithmic system placing individuals into digital proximity with increasingly extreme versions of their existing beliefs, just as geographic sorting places individuals into physical proximity with people who share their worldview.

"The algorithm is the new geography. Like geography, you did not choose it, and you may not be aware of how profoundly it is shaping what you believe."

Digital Proximity and Career Transformation

For individuals with the access and skills to leverage it, digital proximity represents an extraordinary career development tool. A writer who cultivates a large, engaged online following is proximate to a vast potential audience for their work; previously, this required geographic presence in a media capital. A software developer who contributes substantially to a major open-source project achieves a form of professional visibility and community embeddedness that was previously only available to those who could attend the right conferences or work at the right companies.

The democratization of expertise visibility through platforms like GitHub, LinkedIn, Twitter/X, Substack, and YouTube has genuinely expanded the range of individuals who can achieve professional recognition and opportunity, regardless of their physical location. But it has also created new forms of proximity inequality; between those who are algorithmically visible and those who are not, and between those with the skills and resources to cultivate digital community and those without.

Chapter Fourteen: Working the Room. How to Harness Proximity Deliberately

"Once you see the invisible hand of proximity at work, you cannot unsee it. Then you must choose what to do with that knowledge."

The Proximity Audit

The first step toward consciously harnessing proximity is to take honest stock of the proximity environments you currently inhabit. Consider the following dimensions:

Relational proximity: Who are the five to ten people you spend the most time with? What are their ambitions, their habits, their worldviews, their income levels, their health behaviors? Research consistently suggests that you are, on many measurable dimensions, converging toward the average of your proximate community. Are you happy with that average?

Professional proximity: Are you physically or digitally proximate to the leading thinkers, practitioners, and opportunity-creators in your field? Do you attend the conferences, inhabit the communities, and engage with the platforms where the most important conversations in your industry occur? If not, what is preventing you from achieving greater proximity to professional excellence?

Intellectual proximity: What ideas, what content, what communities of discourse are you in regular proximity to? Are they expanding your understanding, challenging your assumptions, and exposing you to the best thinking available? Or are they primarily reinforcing what you already believe?

Physical proximity: Does your physical location give you access to the opportunities, resources, networks, and quality of environment that support the life you want? If not, is this a circumstance that it is within your power to change?

Strategic Relocation

For many people, the single highest-leverage proximity intervention available is geographic relocation. Moving to a city with greater economic opportunity, a larger pool of compatible partners, a more vibrant intellectual community, or a higher quality of schools and environment can transform life outcomes in ways that no amount of self-improvement within a limiting proximity environment can match.

This is not a counsel of rootlessness. The costs of relocation, including the disruption of existing relationships, the loss of community belonging, and the financial and logistical demands of moving, are real and significant. But for people who are systematically limited by the proximity environments of their current location, trapped in labor markets with limited opportunity, in social environments that constrain their development, in political or cultural environments that conflict with their deepest values; for them, deliberate relocation is not running away. It is running toward.

The research on geographic mobility confirms that willingness to relocate for opportunity is a significant predictor of economic advancement. The individuals who achieve the greatest career trajectories are, as a group, those who have been willing to position themselves physically in the environments where the most valuable opportunities exist; those who have chosen their proximity environments strategically rather than simply inheriting them.

Curating Your Social Proximity

If you cannot immediately change your physical location, you can make significant changes to your social proximity. The people you choose to spend time with, the communities you join, the events you attend, and the relationships you invest in are, within the constraints of your physical environment, within your control.

Deliberate community membership, whether joining professional associations, interest groups, athletic clubs, volunteer organizations, alumni networks, or faith communities, is a form of social proximity engineering. It places you in regular, repeated contact with people who share specific values, interests, or goals, creating the conditions for the deep relationships and informal network effects that proximity makes possible.

Mentorship seeking is perhaps the highest-return proximity investment available to anyone at any career stage. The individual who identifies someone operating at the level they aspire to and finds ways to be genuinely proximate to them, to work for them, to assist them, and to engage with their community, gains access to forms of knowledge, standard-setting, and network connection that cannot be replicated through any other means.

One of us learned this lesson from a high school cross country coach in a way that has never been forgotten. Between junior and senior year, the coach called a meeting that had nothing to do with training or race strategy. He sat across his desk, asked who we had been spending time with that summer, and listened carefully as the names came out. He knew almost everyone in the grade, and when the list was finished, he said quietly that he had just heard the names of most of the notable troublemakers in the school. He said he was not sure he wanted that influence on his team. He did not issue an ultimatum. He put the choice where it belonged: in our hands.

The coach was the reigning high school national coach of the year, sponsored by Nike and New Balance. He had built something worth protecting, and he understood, in entirely practical terms, that the social proximity of his athletes shaped the kind of team he could field and the kind of people they would become. He was not moralistic about it. He was precise. He named specific people whose company he recommended instead, people who were going somewhere, who would pull rather than drag. The choice made that fall contributed to a state championship in cross country and, more durably, to a different trajectory in life.

The story illustrates the mechanism more vividly than any data point can: social proximity is not a passive condition you find yourself in. It is an active choice you make, repeatedly, in small decisions about whose company you keep, whose invitations you accept, and whose standards become the ambient standard you are measured against. The coach understood that you become, over time, a composite of the people you spend the most time with. He had seen it happen, in both directions, more times than he could count.

"If you're the smartest person in the room, find another room."

Managing Digital Proximity

In the digital domain, proximity curation requires active, conscious management of the algorithmic environments you inhabit. Default algorithmic proximity, meaning the proximity determined by platforms optimized for engagement, will tend toward radicalization, outrage, and intellectual echo chambers. Deliberately curated digital proximity, comprising the communities, feeds, and content streams you consciously select and invest in, can be a powerful tool for intellectual development and professional growth.

The practices of deliberate digital proximity management include: actively seeking out voices that challenge your existing perspectives; investing in specific communities where the quality of discourse is high and the participants are genuinely expert; reducing exposure to high-volume, low-quality content that merely activates emotional responses without advancing understanding; and participating actively, not just passively, in the digital communities that matter most to your growth.

Teaching Children About Proximity

Perhaps the most important application of the proximity framework is in how we raise and educate children. If we understand that children's outcomes are shaped profoundly by their proximity environments, we bear a responsibility to think carefully about the schools, neighborhoods, communities, and social environments we place them in; and the frameworks we give them to understand their own situation.

Children who understand that they can actively seek out proximity to excellence, including better teachers, inspiring mentors, and more ambitious peers, are equipped with a form of agency that the mythology of pure individual merit does not provide. Rather than waiting for opportunity to find them, they can learn to position themselves in proximity to it. This is not a passive skill. It is an active life strategy.

Conclusion: The Most Important Move You Will Ever Make

"You cannot choose where you are born. But you can choose, with increasing freedom and deliberateness as you grow, where you stand."

We began this book with a simple, perhaps provocative thesis: that proximity (physical, social, intellectual, and digital) is the hidden master variable of human life. We have now examined this thesis across more than a dozen domains of human experience, from the most intimate (whom we love) to the most cosmic (what we believe about God and the universe).

In each domain, the evidence converges on the same conclusion. The partner you married is someone who happened to be in your radius. The education you received is the education your location provided. The career you built was shaped by the networks and clusters your geography gave you access to. The health you enjoy or struggle with is significantly determined by the quality of your environment. The wealth you have or lack reflects, in large measure, the economic geography of your birth and upbringing. The religion you practice is the faith of your neighborhood. The language you think in is the language of your place. The political beliefs you hold are the beliefs of your proximate community.

None of this is fully deterministic. Human agency is real. Individual effort matters. Exceptional people do transcend their proximity circumstances. But they do so against significant headwinds, and their exceptionalism should not be used to deny the structural reality that proximity creates. For every person who escapes a limiting proximity environment through extraordinary individual effort, thousands do not; not because they are less capable or less worthy, but because the headwinds are too strong and the opportunities to redirect their proximity too rare.

"Greatness is not what you were born with. It is what you managed to get near."

The honest acknowledgment of proximity's power is not a counsel of despair. It is the beginning of wisdom. When you understand that your life has been shaped by where you have been, you can begin to ask the transformative question: where should I be?

For some people, the answer is a geographic move: to a city where their ambitions can find expression, where their talents can find a market, where their values can find a community. For others, the answer is a social move; a deliberate investment in relationships with people who operate at a higher level, who have achieved what they aspire to, and who hold standards and expectations that will raise their own. For still others, the answer is an intellectual move: a deliberate expansion of the ideas, perspectives, and communities they engage with, to break the echo chamber and encounter the discomfort that genuine growth requires.

In every case, the answer involves a conscious act of proximity management: the recognition that you are not merely subject to your environment, but capable of choosing and changing it.

This is the ultimate lesson of the proximity thesis. Not fatalism, but agency. Not the crushing weight of circumstance, but the liberating recognition that circumstance can be changed, that environment can be chosen, and that the most powerful investment you can make in your own future is not working harder within a limiting proximity environment, but finding the courage, the strategy, and the resources to change it.

The most important move you will ever make is not the move on a chess board or the move in your career. It is the literal move: the decision to place yourself in proximity to the people, places, ideas, and institutions that will make you who you want to become.

Where you stand determines what you see, what you know, who you meet, and who you become. Stand accordingly.

✦ ✦ ✦

Afterword: The Twelve Principles of Proximity

For ease of reflection and application, here are the twelve core principles developed in this book:

Principle 1: The Radius Principle

You do not search the world for your opportunities, partners, or beliefs. You draw from the pool immediately around you. The quality and size of that pool is the primary determinant of your outcomes.

Principle 2: The Population Principle

Statistical probability, not divine intervention, explains most of your significant encounters. You met your partner because you were both in the same geographic and social radius; the universe did not select you for each other.

Principle 3: The Mere Exposure Principle

Repeated proximity to people, ideas, and institutions increases your affiliation with and appreciation of them. Familiarity, born of proximity, is among the most powerful forces shaping preference and belief.

Principle 4: The Zip Code Principle

Your address is not merely a place to receive mail. It is a determinant of your school quality, your health, your wealth trajectory, your social network, your safety, and your life expectancy.

Principle 5: The Cluster Principle

Excellence, innovation, and opportunity are not uniformly distributed. They cluster in specific places, institutions, and communities. Strategic positioning within those clusters is among the highest-leverage investments available to you.

Principle 6: The Social Contagion Principle

Health behaviors, happiness levels, ambition, and belief are all socially contagious. They spread through networks of physical proximity. You are converging toward the average of those near you.

Principle 7: The Tacit Knowledge Principle

The most valuable knowledge cannot be transmitted digitally. It transfers through proximity: through apprenticeship, mentorship, and the informal exchange that occurs among people sharing physical space over time.

Principle 8: The Geographic Faith Principle

Your religion, your politics, and your deepest moral convictions were largely assigned to you by your proximity to a specific tradition, community, and cultural environment. They are genuine and meaningful; they are also proximity-shaped.

Principle 9: The Contact Principle

Prejudice thrives on distance and diminishes with proximity. The most effective interventions against intergroup prejudice are those that bring different groups into equal-status, cooperative physical contact.

Principle 10: The Serendipity Principle

The most important creative and professional breakthroughs cannot be planned; they can only be enabled. They emerge from the density of proximity, from the accidental encounters that high-quality, diverse physical environments generate.

Principle 11: The Digital Proximity Principle

Digital networks have created new proximity environments with their own geography, determined by algorithms rather than physical space. These environments require conscious curation; default algorithmic proximity serves platform engagement, not human flourishing.

Principle 12: The Agency Principle

Proximity is not destiny. Understanding the power of proximity gives you the most important tool of self-determination: the ability to consciously choose, cultivate, and change the environments that are shaping who you are becoming.

A Note on Sources and Further Reading

The arguments in this book draw on a large body of scholarly research across multiple disciplines, including sociology, economics, public health, psychology, criminology, political science, and urban planning. The following works are among the most important foundations for the ideas presented, and are recommended to readers who wish to explore these arguments in greater depth. Works marked with an asterisk (*) address themes closely related to those of this book and are cited here both as intellectual debts and as points of productive comparison.

Relationships and Social Networks

Christakis, Nicholas A., and James H. Fowler. Connected: The Surprising Power of Our Social Networks and How They Shape Our Lives (2009). The foundational work on the social contagion of health behaviors, emotions, and beliefs through proximity networks.

Rosenfeld, Michael J. How Couples Meet and Stay Together. Stanford University research project tracking how Americans form romantic relationships, consistently demonstrating the primacy of social and geographic proximity.

Education and Opportunity

Chetty, Raj, et al. The Opportunity Atlas: Mapping the Childhood Roots of Social Mobility (2018). A landmark dataset and analysis demonstrating the geographic determinants of economic mobility in the United States.

Gladwell, Malcolm. Outliers: The Story of Success (2008). Accessible exploration of how time, place, and circumstance shape extraordinary achievement; a popular introduction to proximity-adjacent arguments.

Health and Place

Gallagher, Winifred. The Power of Place: How Our Surroundings Shape Our Thoughts, Emotions, and Actions (1993). * An early and important examination of how physical environments affect mood, behavior, and psychological wellbeing, drawing on research in environmental psychology, neuroscience, and biology. While the focus is more biological than sociological, Gallagher anticipates many of the arguments made in later decades about place and human flourishing.

Marmot, Michael. The Status Syndrome: How Social Standing Affects Our Health and Longevity (2004). Comprehensive examination of the social determinants of health, with particular attention to how position in social hierarchies, shaped by geography, affects biological outcomes.

Wilkinson, Richard, and Kate Pickett. The Spirit Level: Why Greater Equality Makes Societies Stronger (2009). Analysis of how income inequality, a geographic and structural variable, shapes health, social trust, and wellbeing across nations and regions.

Cities, Economy, and Innovation

Florida, Richard. The Rise of the Creative Class (2002). Examination of how geographic clustering of creative and intellectual talent drives economic and cultural innovation.

Florida, Richard. Who's Your City? How the Creative Economy Is Making Where to Live the Most Important Decision of Your Life (2008). * Argues that the choice of where to live is as consequential as whom to marry or what career to pursue, and that place exerts decisive influence over professional opportunity, romantic partners, and personal happiness. The book that most directly covers adjacent terrain to this one, grounded in urban economics and regional personality data. Readers who find the proximity thesis compelling are strongly encouraged to read this alongside the present volume.

Glaeser, Edward. Triumph of the City: How Our Greatest Invention Makes Us Richer, Smarter, Greener, Healthier, and Happier (2011). The definitive economic argument for why geographic density and urban proximity are among the most powerful forces in human history.

Moretti, Enrico. The New Geography of Jobs (2012). * A rigorous and important work of labor economics demonstrating that an individual's earnings, career prospects, and standard of living are increasingly determined by the city they live in rather than the degree they hold or the effort they apply. Moretti's research on innovation clusters, wage spillovers, and the divergence between brain-hub cities and struggling communities is among the best empirical foundations available for the economic arguments made in Chapters Three, Five, and Eleven of this book.

Weiner, Eric. The Geography of Genius: A Search for the World's Most Creative Places from Ancient Athens to Silicon Valley (2016). * A lively exploration of the thesis that genius and extraordinary creativity are not primarily individual traits but products of specific times and places. Weiner travels to historical clusters of genius — Athens, Florence, Edinburgh, Vienna, Silicon Valley — and examines the environmental, social, and cultural conditions that produced disproportionate concentrations of breakthrough thinking. Complements the arguments in Chapter Eleven on innovation and serendipity.

Serendipity, Randomness, and Optionality

Taleb, Nassim Nicholas. The Black Swan: The Impact of the Highly Improbable (2007). * A landmark work on the nature of rare, high-impact events and the strategies for surviving and benefiting from them. Taleb's advice to position oneself in dense, active, cross-disciplinary environments to maximize exposure to positive unexpected outcomes is among the most rigorous intellectual foundations available for the serendipity arguments made in Chapter Eleven. Readers who found those arguments compelling are strongly encouraged to follow them here.

Geography, Destiny, and Global Inequality

de Blij, Harm. The Power of Place: Geography, Destiny, and Globalization's Rough Landscape (2008). * A comprehensive argument that geography continues to hold billions of people in its grip despite the rhetoric of globalization and a flat world. De Blij covers language, religion, health, economic opportunity, and urban power through the lens of geographic determinism, organized around three categories of people: globals, locals, and mobals. Readers will find close parallels with Chapters Six, Seven, Four, and Five of this book, though de Blij approaches these themes as a traditional geographer rather than through the framework of individual proximity management.

Politics and Belief

Haidt, Jonathan. The Righteous Mind: Why Good People Are Divided by Politics and Religion (2012). Exploration of the moral psychology underlying political and religious belief, with important implications for understanding how proximate cultural environments shape worldview.

Bishop, Bill. The Big Sort: Why the Clustering of Like-Minded America Is Tearing Us Apart (2008). Documentation of the accelerating geographic sorting of Americans by political identity and its consequences for political polarization.

Crime and Place

Sherman, Lawrence W., et al. Hot Spots of Predatory Crime: Routine Activities and the Criminology of Place (1989). The foundational research establishing the geographic concentration of crime and the primacy of place over individual pathology in criminal outcomes.

Social Psychology and Contact

Allport, Gordon W. The Nature of Prejudice (1954). The classic statement of contact theory, the proximity hypothesis for intergroup relations, which remains among the most replicated and influential findings in social psychology.

PROXIMITY

How Where You Are Determines Who You Become

www.ingramcontent.com/pod-product-compliance
Lightning Source LLC
LaVergne TN
LVHW011048110826
845149LV00015B/3403

9798996337415